After

After

Jane Hirshfield

· POEMS ·

HarperCollinsPublishers

HarperCollins books may be purchased for educational, business, or sales promotional use. For information, please write: Special Markets Department, HarperCollins Publishers, 10 East 53rd Street, New York, NY 10022.

FIRST EDITION

Designed by Laura Kaeppel

Printed on acid-free paper

Library of Congress Cataloging-in-Publication Data
Hirshfield, Jane
    After : poems / Jane Hirshfield.—1st ed.
      p. cm.
    ISBN-10: 0-06-077916-0
    ISBN-13: 978-0-06-077916-0
    I. Title.
PS3558.I694A69 2006
811'.54—dc22   2005050260

06 07 08 09 10 ❖/RRD 10 9 8 7 6 5 4 3 2 1

For Carl

CONTENTS

After Long Silence · 1

Pyracantha and Plum · 2

Flowering Vetch · 3

Theology · 4

Hope: An Assay · 6

To Judgment: An Assay · 7

Those Who Cannot Act · 9

Sheep's Cheese · 10

Beneath the Snow, the Badger's Steady Breathing · 11

Sky: An Assay · 12

Pocket of Fog · 13

Articulation: An Assay · 14

Translucence: An Assay · 15

What Is Usual Is Not What Is Always · 16

The Mountain · 17

Tears: An Assay · 18

Poe: An Assay · 19

The Refusal · 21

Dog and Bear · 22

Downed Branch · 23

Vilnius · 24

"Of": An Assay · 25

"To": An Assay · 26

"And": An Assay · 28

Study of Melon & Insect · 29

A Man Walks Through His Life · 30

A Day Comes · 31

The Double · 32

Not Only Parallel Lines Extend to the Infinite · 34

I Imagine Myself in Time · 35

The Meeting · 36

Wanting More and More to Live Unobserved, Unobserving · 37

The Destination · 38

Late Self-Portrait by Rembrandt · 39

Ryoanji: An Assay · 40

To Opinion · 41

The Woodpecker Keeps Returning · 43

"It is night. It is very dark." · 44

Bonsai · 45

The Promise · 46

The Heat of Autumn · 47

To Wake at 3:00 · 48

Dog Still Barking at Midnight · 49

Two Washings · 50

Termites: An Assay · 51

Envy: An Assay · 52

Hesitation: An Assay · *53*

Once: An Assay · *54*

Burlap Sack · *56*

The Monk Stood Beside a Wheelbarrow · *57*

I Write These Words to Delay · *58*

Seventeen Pebbles · *59*

To Spareness · *65*

"Ah!": An Assay · *67*

Against Certainty · *68*

Jasper, Feldspar, Quartzite · *69*

Instant Glimpsable Only for an Instant · *70*

One Sand Grain Among the Others in Winter Wind · *71*

To Speech · *72*

Possibility: An Assay · *76*

Bad Year · *77*

Serrano Pepper · *78*

This Much Is Promised · *79*

In a Room with Five People, Six Griefs · *80*

Ask Much, the Voice Suggested · *81*

To Gravel: An Assay · *82*

Each Morning My Neighbor Walks Out · *83*

Between the Material World and the World of Feeling · *84*

Red Scarf · *85*

The Bell Zygmunt · *86*

Letter to C. · *87*

The Dead Do Not Want Us Dead · *91*

It Was Like This: You Were Happy · *92*

Acknowledgments · *95*

After

After Long Silence

Politeness fades,

a small anchovy gleam
leaving the upturned pot in the dish rack
after the moon has wandered out of the window.

One of the late freedoms, there in the dark.
The leftover soup put away as well.

Distinctions matter. Whether a goat's
quiet face should be called noble
or indifferent. The difference between a right rigor and pride.

The untranslatable thought must be the most precise.

Yet words are not the end of thought, they are where it begins.

PYRACANTHA AND PLUM

Last autumn's chastened berries still on one tree,
spring blossoms tender, hopeful, on another.
The view from this window
much as it was ten years ago, fifteen.
Yet it seems this morning
a self-portrait both clearer and darker,
as if while I slept some Rembrandt or Brueghel
had walked through the garden, looking hard.

Flowering Vetch

Each of the tragedies can be read
as the tale of a single ripening self,
every character part of one soul.
The comedies can be included in this as well.
Often the flaw is a flaw of self-knowledge;
sometimes greed. For this reason
the comic glint of a school of herring leads to no plot line,
we cannot imagine a tragedy of donkeys or bees.
Before the ordinary realities, ordinary failures:
hunger, coldness, anger, longing, heat.
Yet one day, a thought as small as a vetch flower opens.
After, no longer minding the minor and almost wordless role,
playing the messenger given the letter
everyone knows will arrive too late or ruined by water.
To have stopped by the fig and eaten was not an error, then,
but the reason for going.

THEOLOGY

If the flies did not hurry themselves to the window
they'd still die somewhere.

Other creatures choose the other dimension:

to slip

into a thicket, swim into the shaded, undercut
part of the stream.

My dog would make her tennis ball

disappear into just such a hollow,
pushing it under the water with both paws.
Then dig for it furiously, wildly, until it popped up again.

A game or a theology, I couldn't tell.

The flies might well prefer the dawn-ribboned mouth of a trout,
its crisp and speed,

if they could get there,

though they are not in truth that kind of fly
and preference is not given often in these matters.

A border collie's preference is to do anything entirely,
with the whole attention. This Simone Weil called prayer.
And almost always, her prayers were successful—

the tennis ball

could be summoned again to the surface.

When a friend's new pound dog, diagnosed distempered,
doctored for weeks, crawled under the porch to die, my friend crawled after,
pulled her out, said, "No!",

as if to live were just a simple matter of training.
                              The coy-dog, startled, obeyed.
Now trots out to greet my car when I come to visit.

Only a firefly's evening blinking outside the window,
this miraculous story, but everyone hurries to believe it.

HOPE: AN ASSAY

At 79 my friend says, "I feel differently now.
I thought we could change, now I am not so sure.
We are chimpanzees.
Chimpanzees fighting. I begin to lose my old hope."

How hard he still fights, I think,
still struggling with the nature of human nature, his own and others'.
And I, who have always despaired of change,
see him change and grow hopeful.

To Judgment: An Assay

You change a life
as eating an artichoke changes the taste
of whatever is eaten after.
Yet you are not an artichoke, not a piano or cat—
not objectively present at all—
and what of you a cat possesses is essential but narrow:
to know if the distance between two things can be leapt.
The piano, that good servant,
has none of you in her at all, she lends herself
to what asks; this has been my ambition as well.
Yet a person who has you is like an iron spigot
whose water comes from far-off mountain springs.
Inexhaustible, your confident pronouncements flow,
coldly delicious.
For if judgment hurts the teeth, it doesn't mind,
not judgment. Teeth pass. Pain passes.
Judgment decrees what remains—
the serene judgments of evolution or the judgment
of a boy-king entering Persia: "Burn it," he says,
and it burns. And if a small tear swells the corner
of one eye, it is only the smoke, it is no more to him than a beetle
fleeing the flames of the village with her six-legged children.
The biologist Haldane—in one of his tenderer moments—
judged beetles especially loved by God,
"because He had made so many." For judgment can be tender:
I have seen you carry a fate to its end as softly as a retriever
carries the quail. Yet however much
I admire you at such moments, I cannot love you:

you are too much in me, weighing without pity your own worth.

When I have erased you from me entirely,

disrobed of your measuring adjectives,

stripped from my shoulders and hips each of your nouns,

when the world is horsefly, coal barge, and dawn the color of winter butter—

not *beautiful*, not *cold*, only the color of butter—

then perhaps I will love you. Helpless to not.

As a newborn wolf is helpless: no choice but hunt the wolf milk,

find it sweet.

THOSE WHO CANNOT ACT

"Those who act will suffer,
suffer into truth"—
What Aeschylus omitted:
those who cannot act will suffer too.

The sister banished into exile.
The unnamed dog
soon killed.

Even the bystanders vanish,
one by one,
peripheral, in pain unnoticed while

Sheep's Cheese

In the cellar, sheep's milk cheeses
soak in cold brine.
Once a week, a man comes to turn them.
Sixty pounds lifted like child after child,
lain back re-wrapped
in their cloths on the wooden shelves.
The shelves are nameless, without opinion or varnish.
The wheels are only sheep's milk, not ripening souls.
He sings no lullabye to them. But his arms know the weight.

Beneath the Snow, the Badger's Steady Breathing

Beneath the snow,
     the badger's steady breathing.

He does not count the cold as cold.
He does not call his hunger fate.
His sett is neither large nor small. Not dark.

Closer to tree root than human.

Closer to the wilderness
         than to its saints
who sought to learn from where they'd moved.

A life uninterrupting,
     without want or aspiration.
A persistence.

And yet not meager. Not unfeeling.

—Sharp starlight coming all the way down to the snow.

Sky: An Assay

A hawk flies through it, carrying
a still-twisting snake twice the length of its body.

Radiation, smoke, mosquitoes, the music of Mahler fly through it.

The sky makes room, adjusting its airy shoulders.

Sky doesn't age or remember,
carries neither grudges nor hope.
Every morning is new as the last one, uncreased
as the not quite imaginable first.

From the fate of thunderstorms, hailstorms, fog,
sky learns no lesson,
leaping through any window as soon as it's raised.

In speech, furious or tender,
it's still of passing sky the words are formed.
Whatever sky proposes is out in the open.

Clear even when not,
sky offers no model, no mirror—cloudy or bright—
to the ordinary heart: which is secretive,
rackety, domestic, harboring a wild uninterest in sky's disinterest.

And so we look right past sky, by it, through it,
to what also is moody and alters—
erosive mountains, eclipsable moons, stars distant but death-bound.

POCKET OF FOG

In the yard next door,
a pocket of fog like a small herd of bison
swallows azaleas, koi pond, the red-and-gold koi.

To be undivided must mean not knowing you are.

The fog grazes here, then there,
all morning browsing the shallows,
leaving no footprint between my fate and the mountain's.

ARTICULATION: AN ASSAY

A good argument, etymology instructs,
is many-jointed.
By this measure,
the most expressive of beings must be the giraffe.

Yet the speaking tongue is supple,
untroubled by bone.

What would it be
to take up no position,
to lie on this earth at rest, relieved of proof or change?

Scent of thyme or grass
amid the scent of many herbs and grasses.

Grief unresisted as granite darkened by rain.

Continuous praises most glad, placed against nothing.

But thought is hinge and swerve, is winch,
is folding.

"Reflection,"
we call the mountain in the lake,
whose existence resides in neither stone nor water.

TRANSLUCENCE: AN ASSAY

A dog implausibly large,
with fur the color of rose-quartz, slipped through my sleep.

I have never seen roses that color,
or a vein of quartz move through its fissure on soft-padded feet.
This was sure, though: what she wanted was for me to follow.

She did not look back.
A shadow opened then folded behind her.
I followed as if past a gate latch
sliding closed on its own silent weight.

It was not so very different, really.
More as if the narrator had turned and departed,
abandoned the story,
and each tree, each stone, stood clear in its own full fate.

The dream, like the dog, went on, travelled elsewhere.
Passed by the moment when everything might have been changed.
Passed by the moment of knowing I wanted everything changed.

What Is Usual Is Not What Is Always

What is usual is not what is always.
As sometimes, in old age, hearing comes back.

Footsteps resume their clipped edges,
birds quiet for decades migrate back to the ear.

Where were they? By what route did they return?

A woman mute for years
forms one perfect sentence before she dies.

The bitter young man tires;
the aged one sitting now in his body is tender,
his face carries no regret for his choices.

What is usual is not what is always, the day says again.
It is all it can offer.

Not ungraspable hope, not the consolation of stories.
Only the reminder that there is exception.

The Mountain

One moment, the mountain is clear
in strong morning sunlight. The next, vanished in fog.
I return to Tu Fu, afraid to look up again
from my reading and find in the window moonlight—
but when I do, the fog is still there,
and only the ancient poet's hair has turned gray
while a single wild goose passed him, silently climbing.

Tears: An Assay

A great philosopher is born, walks his lifetime's allotment of footsteps, and dies, but while he is living he has the demeanor and body and voice of a great clown. Each of his propositions is heard, but met with snorts, guffaws, and the wiping of tears of laughter from the eyes. Or perhaps it is the reverse: A great comic is born, walks the earth, and dies. But her demeanor and body and voice are such that people listen gravely, they nod in silence at her words, are moved to weeping by the feelings her thoughts cause to rise. The composition of tears of laughter and tears of grief is not, it seems, the same, though the tongue cannot tell this. Different still the tears of outrage, or the tears that come from a misplaced dust mote, errant eyelash, or flake of soot. Each brought to the earth a great if different pleasure. Each died unsatisfied and angry, though this too is not perceived. And where does the mistake lie, if a mistake is granted at all? In the person who refuses an inescapable fate, or in those who shed at his words their tears of subtly erroneous composition?

POE: AN ASSAY

In "The Gold-Bug," the overt finding of the treasure
is tossed out mid-tale like a bone to a waiting dog.
His stories were not intended for the canine heart that howls inside us,
though he fed it the tidbits it needed to stay near.

What could simply be seen, named, described was not his interest.
Half-close your eyes, he advised, to double the world.
The process of a discovery accomplished was his interest,
its after-savoring his appetite and his pleasure.

While he wrote, the peppered moths
of industrial London were growing darker with an internalized protective soot.

While he wrote, the last illegal slave ships were still coming in.

In his 150-year-old prose there is only one word you might recognize as archaic.

Omission his characteristic gesture;
stepping into the thought that thought cannot enter
his characteristic desire.

While he wrote, the ongoing, quiet famine of laborers paid below costs of housing
and food.

While he wrote, the ongoing, unquiet emptying of the Plains.

These things happened under the culture's floorboards and behind its walls.
These things happened beneath the lids of half-closed eyes.

It is not precisely true that they are absent, though it is true they do not appear.

Whether they were for him
embraced or subsumed in his offered terrors cannot be known.

While he wrote, Turgenev, Goethe,
and this lithe-legged haiku of Issa from the other side of the world:

> Spider,
> do not worry.
> I keep house casually.

In Poe the worry is like the long-cooled lead in Baltimore house-glass,
settled and clear.

The Refusal

The usual stories are of foxes and thick-pelted wolves,
but even a house rat will gnaw off a leg if it must.

Some travel on three legs as swiftly as four.
Swimming is harder,
though my friend's three-legged wolfhound can still catch a rabbit.

Easy to wish the rat well, now it is gone,
I who have stared at the trap for years,
refusing the clear necessity, the dream-command.

Dog and Bear

The air this morning,
blowing between fog and drizzle,

is like a white dog in the snow
who scents a white bear in the snow
who is not there.

Deeper than seeing,
deeper than hearing,
they stand and glare, one at the other.

So many listen lost, in every weather.

The mind has mountains,
Hopkins wrote, against his sadness.

The dog held the bear at bay, that day.

DOWNED BRANCH

I wanted to be intimate to my own life.
What came were
the many eating their way through the tree.

Night of no wind, the grass littered with unripe apples.
The limb fell hard.

It was not
the weight of the apples but the many eating,
even on the ground still eating,
anonymous and steady.

Someone else could name them, genus, species.
Someone else could feel for them affection.

I wanted the intimate knowledge
they had of the tree.
Wanted their simple and ruinous hunger,
made without distinction of the lived-in tree.

VILNIUS

For a long time
I keep the guidebooks out on the table.
In the morning, drinking coffee, I see the spines:
St. Petersburg, Vilnius, Vienna.
Choices pondered but not finally taken.
Behind them—sometimes behind thick fog—the mountain.
If you lived higher up on the mountain,
I find myself thinking, what you would see is
more of everything else, but not the mountain.

"OF": AN ASSAY

Its chain link can be delicate or massive. In the human realm, directional: though one thing also connects to another through "and," this is not the same. Consider: "Science and elephants." "The science of elephants." "The elephants of science." In nature, however, the preposition is bidirectional and equal. The tree that possesses the roots is not different from the root-possessed tree. The flashing red of the hummingbird's crest is the bird; the crust of a bread loaf, the loaf. The interior nonexistent without the external, each part coequal. And so grief too becomes meaningless in that fortunate world.

"To": An Assay

If drawn as a cartoon figure,
you would be leaning always forward, feet blurred
with the multiple lines that convey both momentum and hurry.

Your god is surely Hermes:
messenger, inventor,
who likes to watch the traveller passing the crossroads
in any direction.
Your nemesis? The calm existence of things as they are.

When I speak as here,
in the second person, you are quietly present.
You are present in presents as well, which are given *to*.

Being means and not end, you are mostly modest,
obedient as railroad track to what comes or does not.

Yet your work requires
both transience and transformation:
night changes to day, snow to rain, the shoulder of the living pig to meat.

When attached to verbs, you sometimes change them
to adjectives, adverbs, nouns,
a trick I imagine
would bring enormous pleasure,
were you capable of pleasure. You are not.

You live below the ground of humor, hubris, grievance, grief.
Whatever has been given you,
you carry, indifferent as a planet to your own fate.

Yet it is you,
polite retainer of time and place, who bring us to ours,
who do not leave the house of the body
from the moment of birth until your low-voiced murmur, "dust to dust."

And so we say, *"today," "tomorrow."*
But from yesterday, like us, you have vanished.

"And": An Assay

The strange wind pressed on everything at once—
A door blew open in one room, a vase fell in another.

In this not unlike the word "and": omnipresent even unseen.

Before disappears.
After transforms into others.
"And"—that strong rock—stays standing.

Undevourable *thus* of connection. Even death spits it back.

STUDY OF MELON & INSECT

A small misshapen gourd rests on the whiteness.
Near it a beetle, one wing lifted slightly above the other.

No reason why these.
The painter could have practiced a twisted pine branch housing a heron.
He could have brushed the ten thousand fish as arhats at play.

The two have travelled the centuries together
like the two halves
of a long and unlikely marriage met on a park bench—

Six decades, and still I sometimes find him a stranger,
the old woman pretends to complain.

A Man Walks Through His Life

A man walks through his life
as he did when he was a boy,
taking a pear here, an apple there,
three peaches.

It is easy. They are there, by the roadside.

I want to say to him, stop.
I want to say to him, where is the plum tree you planted?

But how can I say this?
I suck on the pit of my question,
I who also eat daily the labor of others.

A Day Comes

A day comes
when the mouth grows tired
of saying "I."

Yet it is occupied
still by a self which must speak.
Which still desires,
is curious.
Which believes it has also a right.

What to do?
The tongue consults with the teeth
it knows will survive
both mouth and self,

which grin—it is their natural pose—
and say nothing.

The Double

More and more I have come to wonder
about this stranger—
woman whose sweaters and coats resemble my own,

whose taste in breads and coffee
resembles my own,
who sleeps when I sleep, wakens when I awaken.

For her,
whose verb form takes the felicitous *s* at its close,
what happens is simply what happens.

I fret the most slender of errors—
the name forgotten, the borrowed book unreturned—

but never have found her holding a teacup
or coin between her fingers
as if its substance and purpose were something she did not comprehend.

How self-assured she seems,
who decides nothing,
whose insomnia is to my own what the shadow of a leaf is to a leaf.

I am tired, but she is not tired.
I am wordless;
she, who has never spoken a word of her own,
is full of thoughts as precise and impassioned
as the yellow and black exchanges of a wasp's striped body.

For a long time I thought her impostor.
Then realized:
her jokes, even her puns, are only too subtle for me to follow.

And so we go on, mostly ignoring each other,
though what I cook, she eats with seeming gusto,
and letters intended for her alone I open with a curious ease,
as if I, not she, were the long-accomplished thief.

Not Only Parallel Lines Extend to the Infinite

For a few days, any pattern lingers—

Just now, for instance,
though here it is California and late afternoon,
the urge to be drinking bad coffee and eating good butter
on rolls for breakfast at the Hotel Fortuna in Kraków.

Then putting some slices
of brown bread and cheese in a heavy napkin for later.

Flavors vanish first, and then the sounds.
Unphilosophical as a yet unsharpened pencil, the senses;
as without purpose.
A horse's muzzle struck deep in the oats and his eyes half closed.

At each X, the three worlds meet, then part forever.
Of this the horse knows nothing, living outside of time.

And if I, like Chekhov's sleepless coachman,
were to go now and whisper "Kraków" into his ears,
he would greet the sound as only another mystery he cannot obey—
a command neither *canter* nor *carrot*,
though almost familiar, almost a thing he can taste.

I Imagine Myself in Time

I imagine myself in time looking back on myself—
this self, this morning,
drinking her coffee on the first day of a new year
and once again almost unable to move her pen through the iron air.
Perplexed by my life as Midas was in his world of sudden metal,
surprised that it was not as he'd expected, what he had asked.
And that other self, who watches me from the distance of decades,
what will she say? Will she look at me with hatred or with compassion,
I whose choices made her what she will be?

THE MEETING

The rat was fat and healthy and equally surprised,
almost insulted. Leaving only because I was larger
but renouncing no claim.
As I, at times, have looked my fate in the face
and acknowledged nothing.
Continued as if I could, as if this life were mine to choose,
and I the unquestioned lord of my basement kingdom
with its single, high, and unwashed corner window.

WANTING MORE AND MORE
TO LIVE UNOBSERVED, UNOBSERVING

Wanting more and more to live unobserved,
unobserving,
like a dog who takes the bone and goes to another room
where it just fits under the low-legged table or couch.

In the farthest depths, no sunlight reaches.
Yet certain fish, now eyeless, streak with luminescence
when excited;
a lowered bathysphere turns on a floodlight
and is mobbed, the strange-formed bodies drawing in for miles.

No one was ever meant to see this.
Certainly not the fish, who see nothing, whose
tentacles travel the cold light, and no one knows how or why.

Like human beings to a mystery
they imagine feels some passion for their fate.

And the dog? Fallen into the marrow-pleasure completely.

THE DESTINATION

I wanted something, I wanted. I could not have it.
Irremediable rock of refusal, this world thick with bird song,
tender with starfish and apples.
How calming to say, "Turn right at the second corner,"
and be understood,
and see things arrive as they should at their own destination.
Yet we speak in riddles—
"Turn back at the silence." "Pass me the mountain."
To the end we each nod, pretending to understand.

Late Self-Portrait by Rembrandt

The dog, dead for years, keeps coming back in the dream.
We look at each other there with the old joy.
It was always her gift to bring me into the present—

Which sleeps, changes, awakens, dresses, leaves.

Happiness and unhappiness
differ as a bucket hammered from gold differs from one of pressed tin,
this painting proposes.

Each carries the same water, it says.

Ryoanji: An Assay

Wherever a person stands in the garden of Ryoanji, there is always a stone that cannot be seen. It is like the sliver of absence found on the face of a man who has glimpsed in himself a thing until then unknown. Inside the silence, just before he begins to weep. Not because of the thing he has learned—monstrous or saintly, it was always within him—but for the amplitude he hadn't believed was there.

To Opinion

Many capacities have been thought to define the human—
yet finches and wasps use tools; speech comes
into this world in many forms.
Perhaps it is you, Opinion.

Though I cannot know for certain,
I doubt the singing dolphins have opinions.

This thought, of course, is you.

A mosquito's estimation of her meal, however subtle,
is not an opinion. That's my opinion, too.

To think about you is to step into
                                your arms? a thicket? pitfall?

When you come rising strongly in me, I feel myself grow separate
and more lonely.
Even when others share you, this is so.

Darwin said no fact or description that fails to support an argument can serve.

Myōe wrote: *Bright, bright, bright, bright, the moon.*

Last night there were whole minutes when you released me.
Ocean ocean ocean was the sound the sand
made of the moonlit waves
breaking on it.

I felt no argument with any part of my life.

Not even with you, Opinion, who drifted in salt waters with the bullwhip kelp
and phosphorescent plankton,
nibbling my legs and rib cage to remind me where Others end and I begin.

Good joke, I agreed with you, companion Opinion.

The Woodpecker Keeps Returning

The woodpecker keeps returning
to drill the house wall.
Put a pie plate over one place, he chooses another.

There is nothing good to eat there:
he has found in the house
a resonant billboard to post his intentions,
his voluble strength as provider.

But where is the female he drums for? Where?

I ask this, who am myself the ruined siding,
the handsome red-capped bird, the missing mate.

"It is night. It is very dark."

Rainfall past any interrogation.
Questions and answers are not the business of rain.

Yet I step forward by them—
Left foot? Yes. Right foot? Yes.
And all the time wanting to be soaked through,
as the flowers of the apricot that open too early,
in mid-December,
are soaked all the way through their slow petals but do not fall.

The colors only slightly deepen.
The fruit has far to travel.
Left foot by right foot under the hidden stars.

And I?
Unfolded question by question,
like an elephant trained to paint what is in her heart.

BONSAI

One morning beginning to notice
which thoughts pull the spirit out of the body, which return it.
How quietly the abandoned body keens,
like a bonsai maple surrounded by her dropped leaves.
Rain or objects call the forgotten back.
The droplets' placid girth and weight. The table's lack of ambition.
How strange it is that longing, too, becomes a small green bud,
thickening the vacant branch-length in early March.

THE PROMISE

Mysteriously they entered, those few minutes.
Mysteriously, they left.
As if the great dog of confusion guarding my heart,
who is always sleepless, suddenly slept.
It was not any awakening of the large, not so much as that,
only a stepping back from the petty.
I gazed at the range of blue mountains,
I drank from the stream. Tossed in a small stone from the bank.
Whatever direction the fates of my life might travel, I trusted.
Even the greedy direction, even the grieving, trusted.
There was nothing left to be saved from, bliss nor danger.
The dog's tail wagged a little in his dream.

The Heat of Autumn

The heat of autumn
is different from the heat of summer.
One ripens apples, the other turns them to cider.
One is a dock you walk out on,
the other the spine of a thin swimming horse
and the river each day a full measure colder.
A man with cancer leaves his wife for his lover.
Before he goes she straightens his belts in the closet,
rearranges the socks and sweaters inside the dresser
by color. That's autumn heat:
her hand placing silver buckles with silver,
gold buckles with gold, setting each
on the hook it belongs on in a closet soon to be empty,
and calling it pleasure.

To Wake at 3:00

To wake at 3:00
and not want to go back to sleep
is different
from waking and wanting
not to go back to sleep.

Thoughts
come to the mind,
predictable almost as breath.
The day's small errors and failures.
Wrong words that were said,
right ones that were not.

Outside the window
a truck, with yellow lights
running the length of its body
and *R&L Cargo* lettered large down its side,
diesels the street inexplicably backward.

Making its own deliveries,
equally exhausted, from some great distance.

Dog Still Barking at Midnight

It has come to this:
three ants, seemingly separate, seemingly aimless,
wandering a shelf.

They've appeared and disappeared for days between jars and bottles.
Luckless, they move without pausing.

A single breath-puff could send any one to the floor.
How distant they must be from the nest—
yet none consults with another,
none turns to the others for reassurance or warmth.

In their cold bodies: calcium, carbons, a trace of nickel.

Inexhaustible solitude, how did you come so far
to waver on the slim antennae of these my sisters?

Two Washings

One morning in a strange bathroom
a woman tries again and again to wash the sleep
from her eyelids' corners,
until she understands. Ah, she thinks, it begins.
Then goes to put on the soup,
first rerinsing the beans, then lifting the cast-iron pot
back onto the stove with two steadying hands.

Termites: An Assay

So far the house still is standing.
So far the hairline cracks wandering the plaster
still debate, in Socratic unhurry, what constitutes a good life.
An almost readable language.
Like the radio heard while travelling in a foreign country—
you know that something important has happened, but not what.

Envy: An Assay

A mother sings to her infant,
Most beautiful in all the world, and you stand helpless.
Wind outside the window,
looking in with shackled ankles, wrists.
Your fate is to be yourself, both punishment and crime.
Yet you, too, had a mother. Had two sisters.
A photo shows the bone structure's slow shifting:
your face, small, blurred with something almost sorrow,
peers between them.

Hesitation: An Assay

Sometimes only a slowing
so momentary it can scarcely be seen—
as if a dog,
chasing something large and swift and important,
were distracted by the white tremor of an overhead moth.

Other times a full lifetime tentative, lost.

The line of the roof in a child's crayoned drawing
can show a hesitation almost fatal.
The rain
comes to it hard or less hard,
knowing nothing of hesitation's rake-toothed debate.

And the two lovers
now concealed around the corner?
They fool no one, not even themselves,
pausing in their own shadows outside a locked door.

If pleasure requires prolonging, then these lovers.

Yet slowness alone is not to be confused
with the scent of the plum tree just before it opens.

Once: An Assay

Once wakes up in the morning, brews coffee,
       goes outside in its bathrobe to bring the paper from the street.
Once notices the day is possible rain.

At the same time, Once is lightly climbing a tree,
       a tall sycamore
slanting over a late-summer stream.
     A single yellow leaf at once floats down.

A water snake flows one way, the leaf the other.
Once goes with both.
              Then coils in a spring-latched doorknob,
while also swinging its large head around
to scratch the itch that troubles one coarse-haired hip.

Once knows *again* exists
       but this is theoretical knowledge.
Thus Once is ceaselessly tender, though without large passion.

Once doesn't know any better and so loves this world,
in which babies starve, after long enough,
in silence.

Is Once heartless?
       —You may well ask,
who pass your life inside its large, dry hand.

Once turns its face toward the question:
       a horse-shaped clock of bright blue plastic, with red tail.
The dream its whinny wakes you from is also Once's.

This sneeze, this pain, this rage or weeping: one moment only.
Leaving, Once takes in its pocket your slightest sigh.

      Just try to breathe it again, Once murmurs. *You'll see.*

If you protest, it is Once's own and only protest.
If you agree, it is Once that for its instant accedes.

This Möbius is hard to understand but easy to manufacture.
A single strip of paper, turned once, and it's yours.

BURLAP SACK

A person is full of sorrow
the way a burlap sack is full of stones or sand.
We say, "Hand me the sack,"
but we get the weight.
Heavier if left out in the rain.
To think that the sand or stones are the self is an error.
To think that grief is the self is an error.
Self carries grief as a pack mule carries the side bags,
being careful between the trees to leave extra room.
The mule is not the load of ropes and nails and axes.
The self is not the miner nor builder nor driver.
What would it be to take the bride
and leave behind the heavy dowry?
To let the thin-ribbed mule browse in tall grasses,
its long ears waggling like the tails of two happy dogs?

The Monk Stood Beside a Wheelbarrow

The monk stood beside a wheelbarrow, weeping.

God or Buddha nowhere to be seen—
these tears were fully human,
bitter, broken,
falling onto the wheelbarrow's rusty side.

They gathered at its bottom,
where the metal drank them in to make more rust.

You cannot know what you do in this life, what you have done.

The monk stood weeping.
I knew I also had a place on this hard earth.

I Write These Words to Delay

What can I do with these thoughts,
given me as a dog is given her flock?
Or perhaps it is the reverse—
my life the unruly sheep, being herded.
At night,
all lie down on the mountain grasses,
while mirror sheep, a mirror guard-dog
follow one another through rock outcrops,
across narrow streams. They drink and graze by starlight.
This morning, waking to unaccustomed calmness,
I write these words to stay in that silent, unfevered existence,
to delay the other words that are waiting.

After Degas

The woman who will soon
take a lover shaves her legs in the bath,
considering:
Would knowing or not knowing she does this please him more?

Ecstasy: *Czechoslovakia, 1933*

The actress was only seventeen,
and so the director arranged
to have her pricked lightly with pins
at the needed moments.

The Complaint

"I do not like his most recent book,"
one master said of another.
"It compels weeping."

Character and Life

The young novelist held underwater
the head of the character in his book he loved best.
In the book, and as he wrote,
he counted until he was sure it was finished.

Maple

The lake scarlets
the same instant as the maple.
Let others try to say this is not passion.

The Story

"Do you ever _____," my weeping friend asked.
I lied and said yes and invented a story,
a fate I would now have also to live through,
because like a bride I had promised myself to its hands.

Lighthouse

Its vision sweeps its one path
like an aged monk raking a garden,
his question long ago answered or moved on.
Far off, night-grazing horses,
breath scented with oat grass and fennel,
step through it, disappear, step through it, disappear.

Lemon

The grated lemon rind bitters the oil it steeps in.
A wanted flavor.
Like the moment in love when one lover knows
the other could do anything now wanted, yet does not.

Evolution & Glass

For days a fly travelled loudly
from window to window,
until at last it landed on one I could open.
It left without thanks or glancing back,
believing only—quite correctly—in its own persistence.

Tool Use in Animals

For a long time it was thought
the birds were warning: Panther! Panther!
Then someone understood. The birds were scavengers.
The cry was, "Human! Human!"

Global Warming

When his ship first came to Australia,
Cook wrote, the natives
continued fishing, without looking up.
Unable, it seems, to fear what was too large to be comprehended.

The Immortal

This seemingly indestructible head-and-claw
of a handle-less hammer:

a furious, minor god from a great epic,
whose language—camphorous, lithe—was never recorded.

Insomnia, Listening

Three times in one night
a small animal crosses the length of the ceiling.
Each time it goes all the way one way,
all the way back, without hesitation or pause.

Envy that sureness.

It is like being cut-flowers, between the field and the vase.

Why Bodhidharma Went to Motel 6

"Where is your home?" the interviewer asked him.

"Here."

"No, no," the interviewer said, thinking it a problem of translation,
"when you are where you actually live?"

Now it was his turn to think, *Perhaps the translation?*

A Class Almost Empty

How did Roget decide
that the opposite of "time" is not
"instantaneity" but "neverness"—
a concept so difficult he could
scarcely think of additional entries,
resorting instead to phrases from Latin and Greek,
too early for the possibility "Birkenau-Auschwitz."

Sentence

The body of a starving horse cannot forget the size it was born to.

To Sneezing

Pure master of all our losses,
dissolver of self and its zeals—
we bow before you as newspaper bows to the match.

To Spareness

You lean toward nonexistence,
but have not yet become it entirely.
For this reason, you can still be praised.

The tree unleafing enters your dominion.
An early snowfall shows you abide in all things.

Your two dimensions are line and inclination.
Therefore desire,
though it incinders each mote of its object, itself is spare.

The late paintings of Turner
prove your slender depths without limit.
The beauty too of shakuhachi and cello.

"Winter darkness. Rain. No crickets singing."
—You are there, pulling hard on the rope-end.

Remembering you, I remember also compassion.
I cannot explain this.
Nor how you live in a teabowl
or in a stone that has spent a long time in a river.
Nor the way you at times can signal your own contradiction,
meaning *extra*, but not by much—
"Brother, can you spare a dime," one thin man asks of another.

Any room, however cluttered, gestures toward you,
declaring:

"Here lives this, not that."
In mathematics, the modest "<" sign gestures toward you.

Your season is surely November,
your fruit, persimmons ripening by coldness.

Your sound a crow cry, a bus idling at night by roadside.

Without apparent effect,
and so you remind of starlight on the colors of a cow's hide.

Your proposition, like you, is simple, of interest only to the human soul:
　　vast reach of all that is not, and still something is.

"Ah!": An Assay

When the Greek gods would slip into the clothing and bodies of humans, it was not always as it appeared—not always, that is, for seduction, nor to test the warmth of welcome given to strangers. The sex—like the sudden unveiling and recognition—was not without pleasure. But later, they would remember: "The barley soup offered one night in the village of _____, its wild marjoram, scent of scorched iron, and carrots." "Ah!, and the ones who turned away from us, how their eyes would narrow and wrinkle the tops of their noses." "The barnyard odors." "And afterward, sleep in that salt-scent, close by their manure hoards and feathers." "Sleep itself!" "Ah!"

For this soft "ah!," immortals entered the world of bodies.

AGAINST CERTAINTY

There is something out in the dark that wants to correct us.
Each time I think "this," it answers "that."
Answers hard, in the heart-grammar's strictness.

If I then say "that," it too is taken away.

Between certainty and the real, an ancient enmity.
When the cat waits in the path-hedge,
no cell of her body is not waiting.
This is how she is able so completely to disappear.

I would like to enter the silence portion as she does.

To live amid the great vanishing as a cat must live,
one shadow fully at ease inside another.

JASPER, FELDSPAR, QUARTZITE

Jasper, feldspar, quartzite, agate, granite, sandstone, slate.

Some can be rounded, some not.
Some can be flaked, some not.

A person, too, holds her lines of possible fracture.

Snow falls over the cities and mountains.
Cries of the late geese pass through it,
forsythia blossoms far inside their buds.

Each pebble, each planet, gives off a recordable singing.
I have heard them.
Monastic the strangeness.

Perhaps, though, that is the only destination—
beauty & strangeness.
Whose notes abandon the instruments that make them.

Instant Glimpsable Only for an Instant

Moment. Moment. Moment.

—equal inside you, moment,
the velocitous mountains and cities rising and falling,
songs of children, iridescence even of beetles.

It is not you the locust can strip of all leaf.

Untouchable green at the center,
the wolf too lopes past you and through you as he eats.

Insult to mourn you, you who mourn no one, unable.

Without transformation,
yours the role of the chorus, to whom nothing happens.
The living step forward: choosing to enter, to lose.

I, who am made of you only,
speak these words against your unmasterable instruction—

A knife cannot cut itself open,
yet you ask me both to be you and to know you.

One Sand Grain Among the Others in Winter Wind

I wake with my hand held over the place of grief in my body.
"Depend on nothing," the voice advises, but even that is useless.
My ears are useless, my familiar and intimate tongue.
My protecting hand is useless, that wants to hold the single leaf to the tree
and say, *Not this one, this one will be saved.*

To Speech

This first, this last:
there's nothing you wouldn't say.

Unshockable inclusion your most pure nature,
and so you are like an iron pot—
whatever's put in, it holds.

We think it's the fire that cooks the stew,
but speech, it's also you:
teacher
of fire-making and stew-making,
orator of all our plans and intentions.

We think we think with a self.
That also, it seems, is mostly you—
sometimes a single spider's thread of you,
sometimes a mountain.

The late sun paints orange
the white belly of a hawk overhead—
that wasn't you,
though now and here, it is.

If a hungry child says "orange," her taste buds grow larger.

If a person undamaged says "hungry child,"
his despondence grows larger.

You are not, of course, omnipotent.
In fact, you do little unaided by muscle, by matter.
And still, present and absent, speech, you change us.

As Issa changed, writing after the death of his daughter,

> *This world of dew*
> *is a world of dew.*
> *And yet.*

How much of you
was left uninvited into those lines.
That silence your shadow, bringing his grieving to me.

For days
I made phone calls to strangers,
the few words repeated over and over,
between the "please, if you have a moment" and "thank you."

I didn't expect to make a difference, and didn't. And yet.

Your vehicles are air and memory,
teeth, tongue, papyrus, woodblocks, poured lead,
signing fingers, circuits, transistors, and ink.
A wheel is not your vehicle, nor an engine.

Terence was your vehicle,
saying in Latin:
"Whatever is human cannot be foreign to me."

Your own truth as well—
For of all our parts, you are our closest mirror,
growing thin or fat, muscular, clumsy,
speeding or slowing as we do.

The wolf-child without you called wolf-child, not-fully-human.

You are held, in the forms we can know you,
only by creatures
able to pass you to others
living often in sadness and tiredness, sometimes in hope.

A friend, who is sometimes sad, said this:
"To be able to hope means also that we can regret."

You rest, fierce speech, in both.
As well as in bargaining, persuasion, argument, gossip,
flirtation, jokes.

Fear, hunger, rage stammer beyond you:
what lives in words is what words were needed to learn.

And so it is good we sometimes set you down
and walk—

unthinking and peaceful, planning nothing—
by the cold, salt, unobedient, unlistening sea.

Only then, without you, are we able to see you completely,
like those wandering monks
who, calling nowhere home, are everywhere home.

POSSIBILITY: AN ASSAY

Again I looked out the window.
All around me, the morning still dark.

The mountain's outline there, but not the mountain.

Then a neighbor's facing plate-glass filled
with the colors, acute and tender, of a Flemish painting.
Corals, blues.

Which seemed to be a preview of the future but were,
I knew, this moment simply looking elsewhere,
like a woman who has wept for weeks who realizes
that she is also hungry.

BAD YEAR

Even in this bad year,
the apples grow heavy and round.
Three friends and I trade stories:
biopsy, miscarriage, solitude,
a parent's unravelling body or mind.
What is reliable? What do you hold?
I demand of the future, later.
The future—whose discretion is perfect—
says nothing, but rolls another
apple loose from its grip.
A hopeful yellow jacket comes to hunt
the crack, the point of easy entry.

Serrano Pepper

Grief as with the serrano pepper:
first there is actual flavor, then only heat.
What predator insect or mammal, what
backward-leaning desire,
was such blinding meant to protect from?
The self can be seared away, can be taken.
The hoarded honeys and angers, the very names, taken.
One moment: the hoof of the horse propped up, at rest.
Then the next.

THIS MUCH IS PROMISED

Anna Kamieńska, when you prayed
for what you were sure would be granted, you prayed for this:
a life of much suffering.

Reading your words, why do the heart's scales shift?

It is not the gladness of chickens, content to enter the night-coop.

Rather the shocked happiness
of the child who wakes one morning alone, knowing herself abandoned,
and makes breakfast, dresses neatly, sets out for school.
Learns to forge notes from home.

It goes on this way for weeks.

And though they will take her back,
find in another city a lost great-aunt or older cousin,
she does not forget.

Let others imagine those hours as frightened, as lonely.
Asked, she says nothing.

That child's silence, Anna Kamieńska, calm as unmined iron,
I offer you here, next to your own.
I set it beside your trapped bumblebee, your untranslatable window.

In a Room with Five People, Six Griefs

In a room with five people, six griefs.

Some you will hear of, some not.

Let the room hold them, their fears, their anger.

Let there be walls and windows, a ceiling.

A door through which time

changer of everything

can enter.

Ask Much, the Voice Suggested

Ask much, the voice suggested, and I startled.
Feeling my body like the trembling body of a horse
tied to its tree while the strange noise
passes over its ears.
I who in extremity had always wanted less,
even of eating, of sleeping.
Agile, the voice did not speak again, but waited.
"Want more"—
a cure for longing I had not thought of.
But that is how it is with wells.
Whatever is taken refills to the steady level.
The voice agreed, though softly, to quiet the feet of the horse:
A cup taken out, a cup reappears; a bucketful taken, a bucket.

To Gravel: An Assay

In you, as in a life, the part cannot stand for the whole.

One chip of you bites the hand like a word
scissored out of its sentence, without power to help or to harm.

Aggregation is not mathematics—a crowd
not the sum of its persons,
a building not the calculus of its brick;
a teaspoon of you is not yet you, though a single salt flake is salt.

Your philosophy is surely Linnaean, a simple sorting.

Your unit of measure and meditation is weight.

Yet being part air, you can be poured:
for a moment an arc,
a lip, sheers from the truck-bed, glittering like water.

But neither translucent
nor tender toward what you touch, you are not like water.
You are like breath—

a woman sits by the hospital night-bed hearing the difference
between one and many:
a single one of either of you is everything,
a single one of either of you is nothing at all.

Each Morning My Neighbor Walks Out

In the morning
my neighbor walks onto his deck and looks out,
some days in a yellow jacket,
some days in a raincoat, some days in a shirt.
The house is far enough off
I do not know his name, cannot quite see his face.
I would not know him in line at the grocery.
He looks for a moment in my direction, across the small gorge,
then turns and reenters his door.
Between us leaves shift their colors, fall, reappear.
Between us the flash of a bluejay, sometimes a hawk.
Each time happiness greatens, sorrows too must increase,
but I cannot let go the longing for what passes.

BETWEEN THE MATERIAL WORLD
AND THE WORLD OF FEELING

Between the material world and the world of feeling there must be a border—on one side, the person grieves and the cells of the body grieve also; the molecules also; the atoms. Of this there are many proofs. On the other, the iron will of the earth goes on. The torture-broken femur continues to heal even in the last hour, perhaps beyond; the wool coat left behind does not mourn the loss of its master. And yet Cavafy wrote, "In me now everything is turned into feeling—furniture, streets." And Saba found in a bleating goat his own and all beings' sorrow, and this morning the voice of that long-dead goat—which is only, after all, a few black-inked words— cries and cries in my ears. Rilke, too, believed the object longs to awaken in us. But I long for the calm acceptance of a bentwood chair and envy the blue-green curve of a vase's shoulder, which holds whatever is placed within it—the living flower or the dead—with an equally tender balance, and knows no difference between them.

Red Scarf

The red scarf
still hangs over the chairback.
In its folds,
like a perfume
that cannot be quite remembered,
inconceivable *before*.

for L.B. (1950–2004)

The Bell Zygmunt

For fertility, a new bride is lifted to touch it with her left hand,
or possibly kiss it.
The sound close in, my friend told me later, is almost silent.

At ten kilometers, even those who have never heard it know what it is.

If you stand near during thunder, she said,
you will hear a reply.

Six weeks and six days from the phone's small ringing,
replying was over.

She who cooked lamb and loved wine and wild-mushroom pastas.
She who when I saw her last was silent as the great Zygmunt mostly is,
a ventilator's clapper between her dry lips.

Because I could, I spoke. She laid her palm on my cheek to answer.
And soon again, to say it was time to leave.

I put my lips near the place a tube went into
the back of one hand.
The kiss—as if it knew what I did not yet—both full and formal.

As one would kiss the ring of a cardinal, or the rim
of that cold iron bell, whose speech can mean "Great joy,"
or—equally—"The city is burning. Come."

Letter to C.

Your own writings began, you said,
with a path turned away from.
An unnamed girl in a forest, a snake killed with a stone.

But the trajectory of witness inscribes a circle.
For eight decades, the girl looked back at you, along with the others,
vanished and not.

And you?
Late, you saw yourself Orpheus.

Defeated by his own gaze, continuing to sing.

II.

Living memory holds the dead as a hand holds water,
as a dry window keeps the traces of rain.
And still we speak.

I write in these lines what I hear myself saying to others—

that you wanted most, it seemed, to preserve
the dresses and potions of women, an unmetaphysical spider and cat.
Against the age's erasures
praising a blacksmith's forge, a dish of olives set on a table.

Other writers you praised by rebuking,
though I recall no complaint against Whitman,
whose capacious lists and tenderness must have seemed
to you the path of a mirroring soul, if less singed by self-judgment.

This did not keep you from forming your theory—
Whitman's poetry as one cause of the First World War.
Incomprehensible to Americans, obvious to a Lithuanian Pole.

III.

A theology of faith requires acceptance.

Yet transience harrowed you,
as it does whoever loves what exists only in time, in place.
In Paris, Szetejnie, Warsaw, Vilnius, Berkeley.

In certain realms also of hell,
whose ashes darkened the water you leaned to drink.
Beneath your face, a trout's expressionless watching.
Beside it, a dragonfly's wing, inside a cloud.

Near the end, you could not lift your head,
but offered a visitor this:

                    "At least I am conscious.
I have been arguing all morning with your Puritans, I must tell you,
in their strange hats."

It is good to think you fought to the last with those who would narrow the mind.

I cannot remember now your opinion of Milton,
but I think the beauty of his Lucifer, falling and arguing back,
is not dissimilar to your own.

IV.

We sat outside your house on Grizzly Peak,
looking at phrases from Schopenhauer,
a *Tygodnik Powszechny* holding your poems, cartoons in a new *New Yorker*.

A half-timbered cottage from the Brothers Grimm,
steps spiralling down in rough-laid, unmatched stones, hiding its wolf.
Who liked laughter, eating, the hour of the evening cocktail.

Then in a Kraków apartment,
turning for you a book whose pages
showed Lithuanian countryside; you in your eighties; Carol.
Your undiminished amazement—
no matter the houses had vanished, the curve of the river remained.

I long believed ironical your claim it is wrong to love this world as it is.
Then understood. I was mistaken.

And now I cannot ask you: How did you live?

V.

Round cheeses of cows' and of sheep's milk,
wild mushrooms, roast lamb with garlic, red wine:
in Poland, as in Mexico, one feasts by the graveside in autumn.
Laid out on plates, in glassware,
set down on its own mowed grasses, the consumable portions of earth.
What we offer the dead, we offer not them, but ourselves.
You would wish us, I think, less longing.

You studied Shakyamuni's teachings
because he also could not turn his face from suffering,
though for you liberation required
a soul—singular, real, believing beyond any proof that it will last.

Your immutable *"Why?"* remained, like Job's, unanswered.
And still in the halls of silence it echoes again.

Words cannot reach you. Orpheus played no lyre as he walked.
Yet they come—
offering, in earlier, Sanskrit version,
the invocation spoken in Polish throughout your own poems:

> *Gate gate paragate parasamgate bodhi svaha*

"Gone now, released one, far past returning, freed one, suffer no more."

THE DEAD DO NOT WANT US DEAD

The dead do not want us dead;
such petty errors are left for the living.
Nor do they want our mourning.
No gift to them—not rage, not weeping.
Return one of them, any one of them, to the earth,
and look: such foolish skipping,
such telling of bad jokes, such feasting!
Even a cucumber, even a single anise seed: feasting.

September 15, 2001

It Was Like This: You Were Happy

It was like this:
you were happy, then you were sad,
then happy again, then not.

It went on.
You were innocent or you were guilty.
Actions were taken, or not.

At times you spoke, at other times you were silent.
Mostly, it seems you were silent—what could you say?

Now it is almost over.

Like a lover, your life bends down and kisses your life.

It does this not in forgiveness—
between you, there is nothing to forgive—
but with the simple nod of a baker at the moment
he sees the bread is finished with transformation.

Eating, too, is a thing now only for others.

It doesn't matter what they will make of you
or your days: they will be wrong,
they will miss the wrong woman, miss the wrong man,
all the stories they tell will be tales of their own invention.

Your story was this: you were happy, then you were sad,
you slept, you awakened.
Sometimes you ate roasted chestnuts, sometimes persimmons.

ACKNOWLEDGMENTS

The author gratefully thanks the publications in which many of these poems first appeared, sometimes in different versions:

The American Poetry Review: "After Long Silence," "Ask Much, the Voice Suggested," "Between the Material World and the World of Feeling," "The Destination," "The Heat of Autumn," "Hesitation: An Assay," "I Imagine Myself in Time," "I Write These Words to Delay," "'It is night. It is very dark,'" "The Meeting," "The Promise," "The Refusal," "Theology," "Two Washings"

The American Scholar: "'Of': An Assay," "To Gravel: An Assay," "The Woodpecker Keeps Returning"

Atlanta Review: "Envy: An Assay," "Not Only Parallel Lines Extend to the Infinite," "Ryoanji: An Assay"

The Atlantic Monthly: "The Bell Zygmunt," "Pyracantha and Plum"

Columbia Journal: "Downed Branch," "Flowering Vetch"

Forward: "Translucence: An Assay"

The Georgia Review: "'Ah!': An Assay," "'And': An Assay," "Evolution & Glass," "Global Warming," "Lighthouse," "Tears: An Assay," "To Sneezing," "Tool Use in Animals"

Green Mountains Review: "'To': An Assay"

The Kenyon Review: "After Degas," "Character and Life," "A Class Almost Empty," "The Complaint," *Ecstasy:* Czechoslovakia, 1933," "Insomnia, Listening," "Lemon," "Sentence," "Why Bodhidharma Went to Motel 6"

Literary Imagination: "Against Certainty," "One Sand Grain Among the Others in Winter Wind"

Lyric: "Study of Melon & Insect"

MiPoesias: "The Immortal," "Pocket of Fog"

New England Review: "Dog Still Barking at Midnight," "In a Room with Five People, Six Griefs," "Vilnius," "What Is Usual Is Not What Is Always"

New Letters: "Red Scarf," "Sky: An Assay"

The New Yorker: "It Was Like This: You Were Happy"

Nightsun: "Bad Year," "Dog and Bear"

Orion: "Beneath the Snow, the Badger's Steady Breathing," "A Man Walks Through His Life," "Sheep's Cheese"

Ploughshares: "Bonsai," "Each Morning My Neighbor Walks Out," "The Mountain," "Termites: An Assay"

Poetry: "Instant Glimpsable Only for an Instant," "To Judgment: An Assay," "To Spareness"

The Princeton University Library Chronicle: "The Double"

Runes: "Burlap Sack"

Shambhala Sun: "Lighthouse," "The Monk Stood Beside a Wheelbarrow," "Serrano Pepper"

Slate: "Late Self-Portrait by Rembrandt," "Possibility: An Assay," "To Opinion"

Speakeasy: "Maple"

The Threepenny Review: "A Day Comes," "Letter to C.," "Poe: An Assay"

Tin House: "The Story"

Tricycle: "The Dead Do Not Want Us Dead"

TriQuarterly: "Articulation: An Assay," "This Much Is Promised"

Vallum: "Jasper, Feldspar, Quartzite"

Water-Stone Review: "Once: An Assay," "To Speech," "Wanting More and More to Live Unobserved, Unobserving"

The author also gratefully acknowledges the following publications for reprinting poems in this book that first appeared elsewhere: *divide, Island* (Australia), *Island* (Scotland), Poetry Daily (website: www.poems.com), *Shambhala Sun, The Stony Thursday Book* (Ireland), *Tricycle*, and *Urthona* (Great Britain).

Anthologies: *Against Certainty: Poets for Peace Anthology* (Chapiteau Press): "Against Certainty," "The Dead Do Not Want Us Dead"; *America Zen: A Gathering of Poets* (Bottom Dog Press): "The Dead Do Not Want Us Dead," "It Was Like This: You Were Happy," "The Monk Stood Beside a Wheelbarrow," "To Judgment: An Assay"; *The Best American Poetry 2004* (Scribner): "Poe: An Assay"; *The Best American Poetry 2005* (Scribner): "Burlap Sack"; *Manthology* (University of Iowa Press): "A Man Walks Through His Life," "The Monk Stood Beside a Wheelbarrow," "Ryoanji: An Assay"; *Poets Against the War* (Nation Books): "The Dead Do Not Want Us Dead"; *The Wisdom Anthology of North American Buddhist Poetry* (Wisdom Books): "After Long Silence," "Against Certainty," "The Dead Do Not Want Us Dead," "Lighthouse," "Theology," "Why Bodhidharma Went to Motel 6."

A number of the poems included in this book appear in a limited-edition fine press book, *Pebbles & Assays* (Waldron Island, WA: Brooding Heron Press, 2005).

My deep gratitude to the Academy of American Poets and the National Endowment for the Arts for the support of fellowships in poetry, and to Yaddo, the Key West Literary Seminar, and the Vermont Studio Center, under whose hospitality many of the poems in this collection were written.

About the Author

Jane Hirshfield's books of poetry include *After; Given Sugar, Given Salt; The Lives of the Heart; The October Palace; Of Gravity & Angels;* and *Alaya.* She is also the author of a collection of essays, *Nine Gates: Entering the Mind of Poetry,* and editor and co-translator of three collections, *Women in Praise of the Sacred: 43 Centuries of Spiritual Poetry by Women; The Ink Dark Moon: Love Poems by Ono no Komachi and Izumi Shikibu, Women of the Ancient Court of Japan;* and *Mirabai: Ecstatic Poems.* A finalist for the National Book Critics Circle Award and winner of the Poetry Center Book Award, the Northern California Book Award, and fellowships from the Academy of American Poets, National Endowment for the Arts, and Guggenheim and Rockefeller foundations, Hirshfield's work has appeared in *The Best American Poetry, The Pushcart Prize Anthology,* the *New Yorker,* the *Atlantic Monthly, Poetry, Slate, Orion,* and *The American Poetry Review.* A resident of the San Francisco Bay Area, she has taught at the University of California, Berkeley; at the University of Cincinnati; and in Bennington College's MFA Writing Seminars.